Knitting

journal

_____

_____

_____

INDEX

Name	For	Project No.

Project Name _____

Project No.

Who I'm making it for _____

Occasion _____

Date started _____ Date finished _____

SKETCH

NOTES

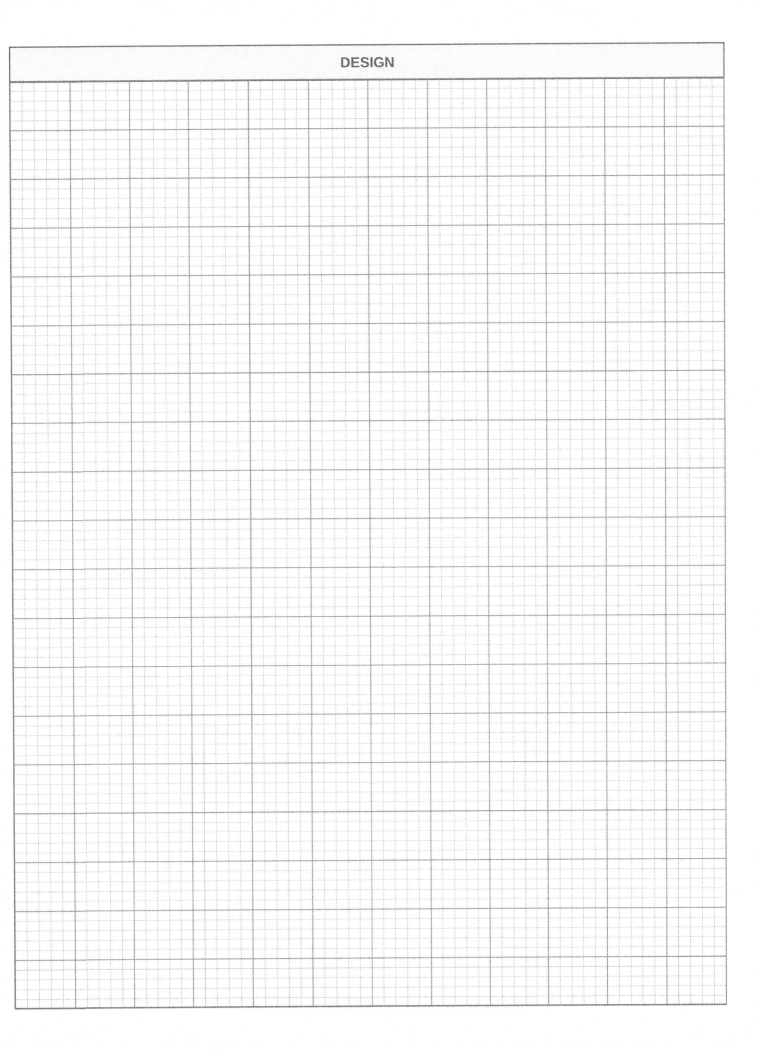

DESIGN

Project Name _____

Project No.

Who I'm making it for _____

Occasion _____

Date started _____ Date finished _____

SKETCH

NOTES

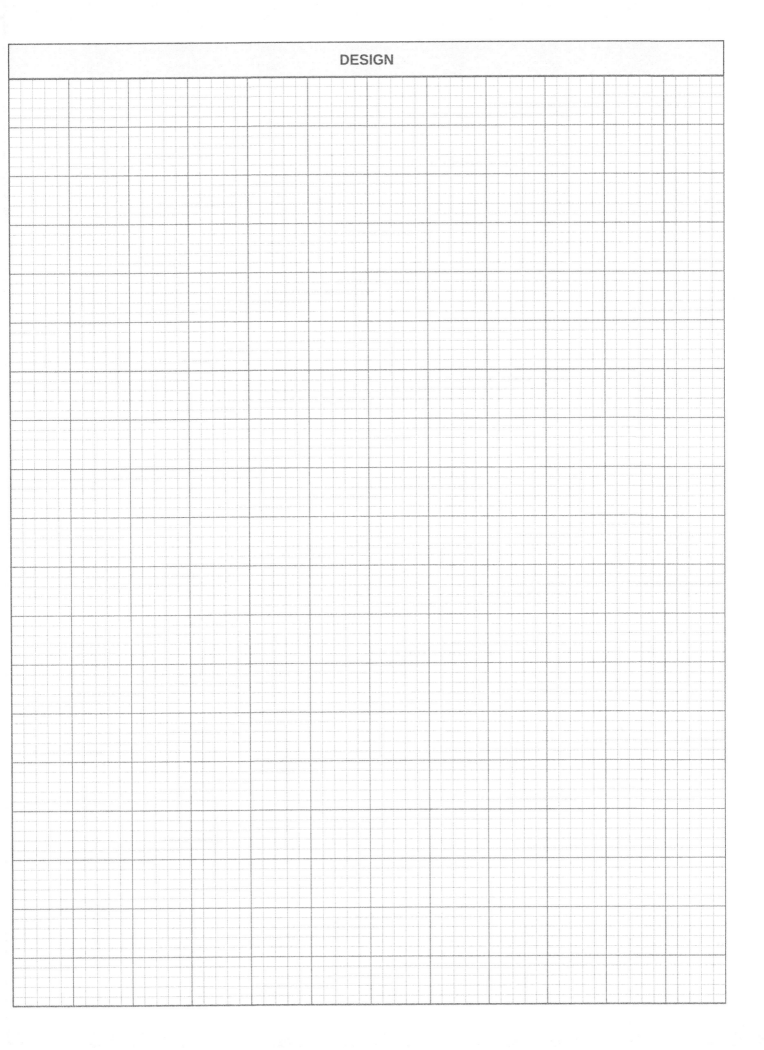

Project Name _____

Project No.

Who I'm making it for _____

Occasion _____

Date started _____ Date finished _____

SKETCH

NOTES

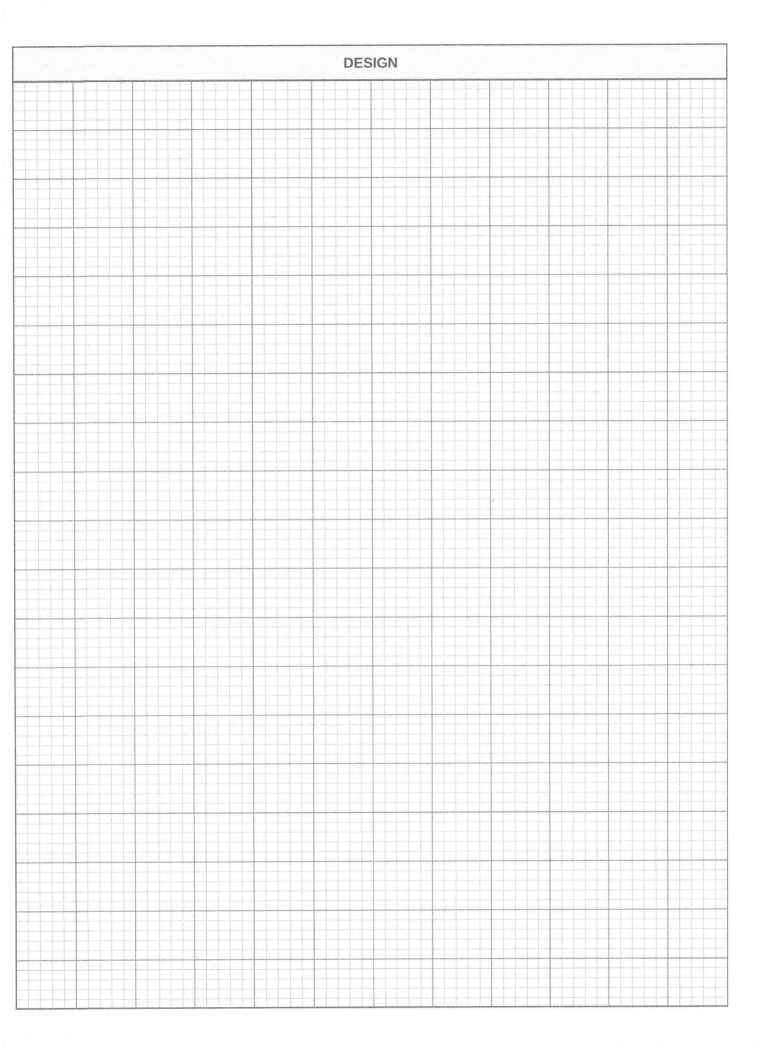

Project Name _____

Project No.

Who I'm making it for _____

Occasion _____

Date started _____ Date finished _____

SKETCH

NOTES

Project Name _____

Project No.

Who I'm making it for _____

Occasion _____

Date started _____ Date finished _____

SKETCH

NOTES

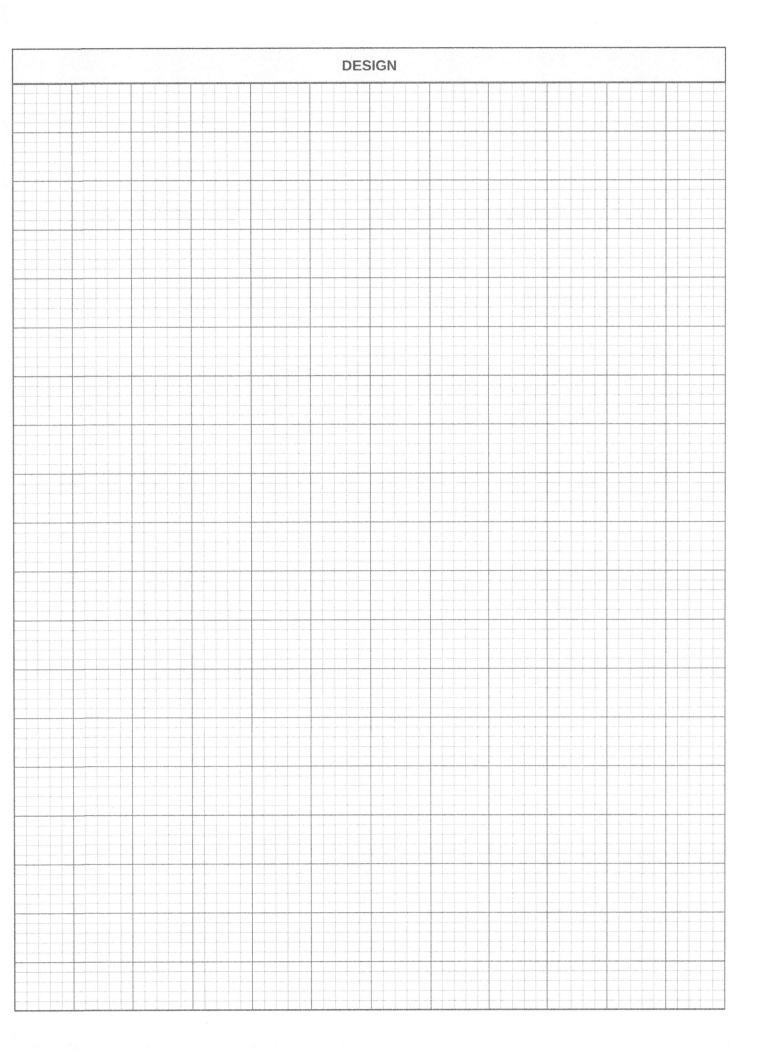

Project Name _____

Who I'm making it for _____

Occasion _____

Date started _____ Date finished _____

Project No.

SKETCH

NOTES

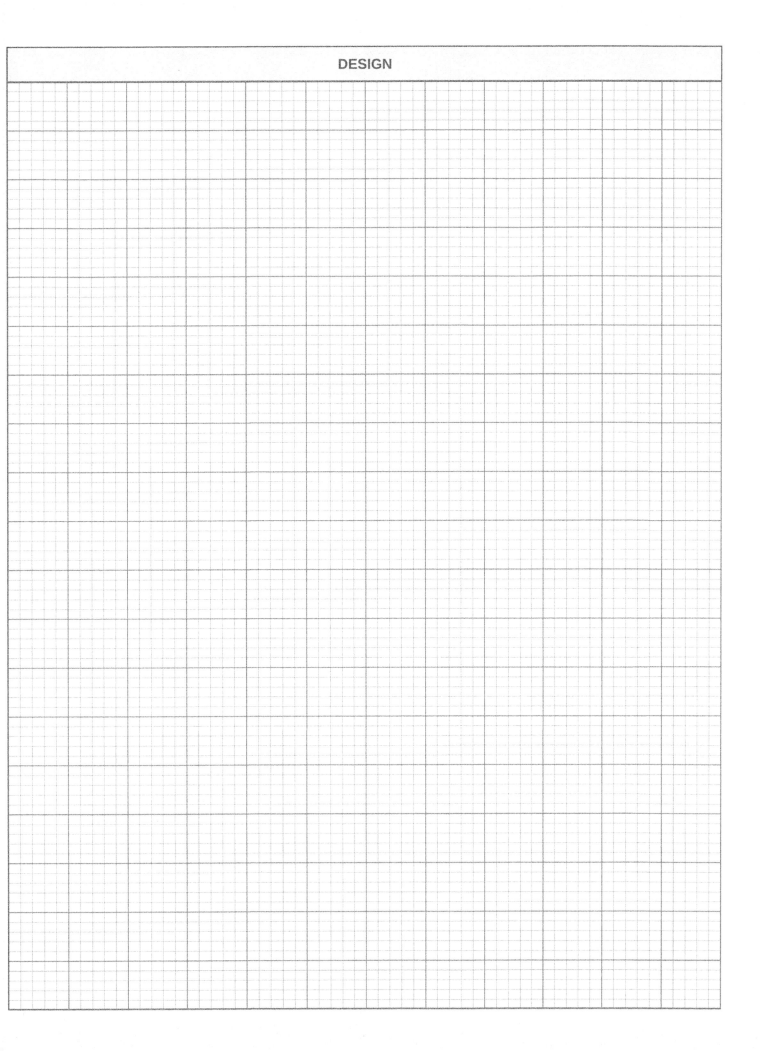

DESIGN

Project Name _____

Project No.

Who I'm making it for _____

Occasion _____

Date started _____   Date finished _____

SKETCH

NOTES

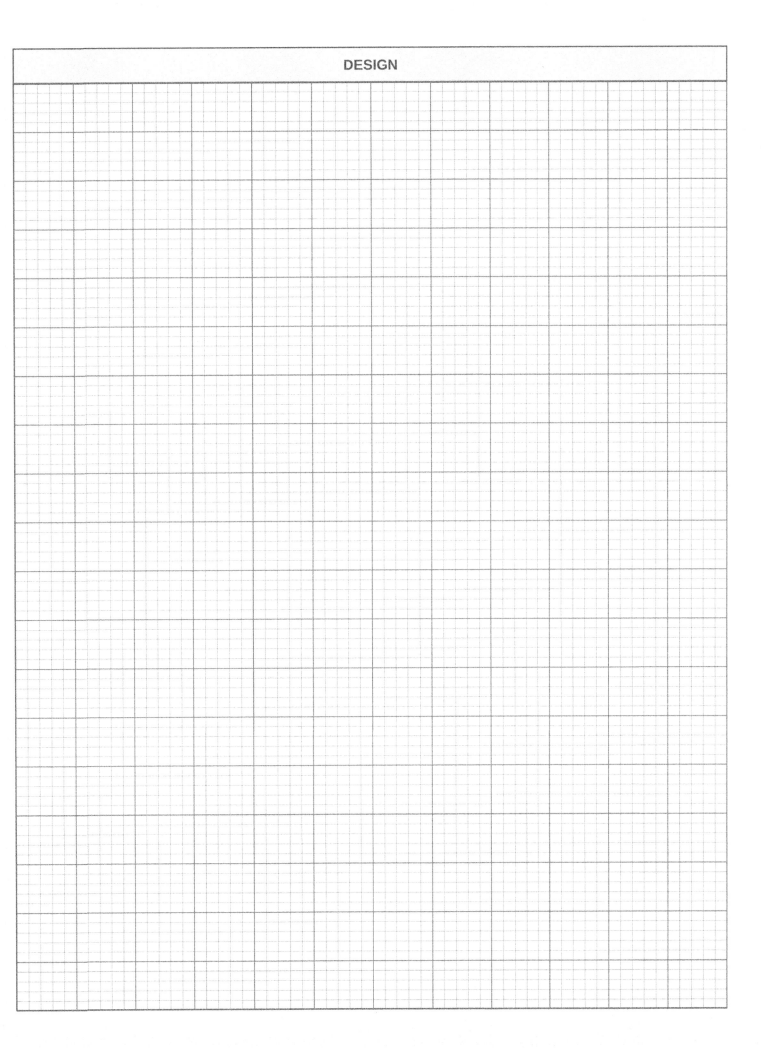

Project Name _____

Who I'm making it for _____

Occasion _____

Date started _____ Date finished _____

Project No.

SKETCH

NOTES

Project Name _____

Project No.

Who I'm making it for _____

Occasion _____

Date started _____ Date finished _____

SKETCH

NOTES

Project Name _____

Project No.

Who I'm making it for _____

Occasion _____

Date started _____ Date finished _____

SKETCH

NOTES

Project Name _____

Who I'm making it for _____

Occasion _____

Date started _____   Date finished _____

SKETCH

NOTES

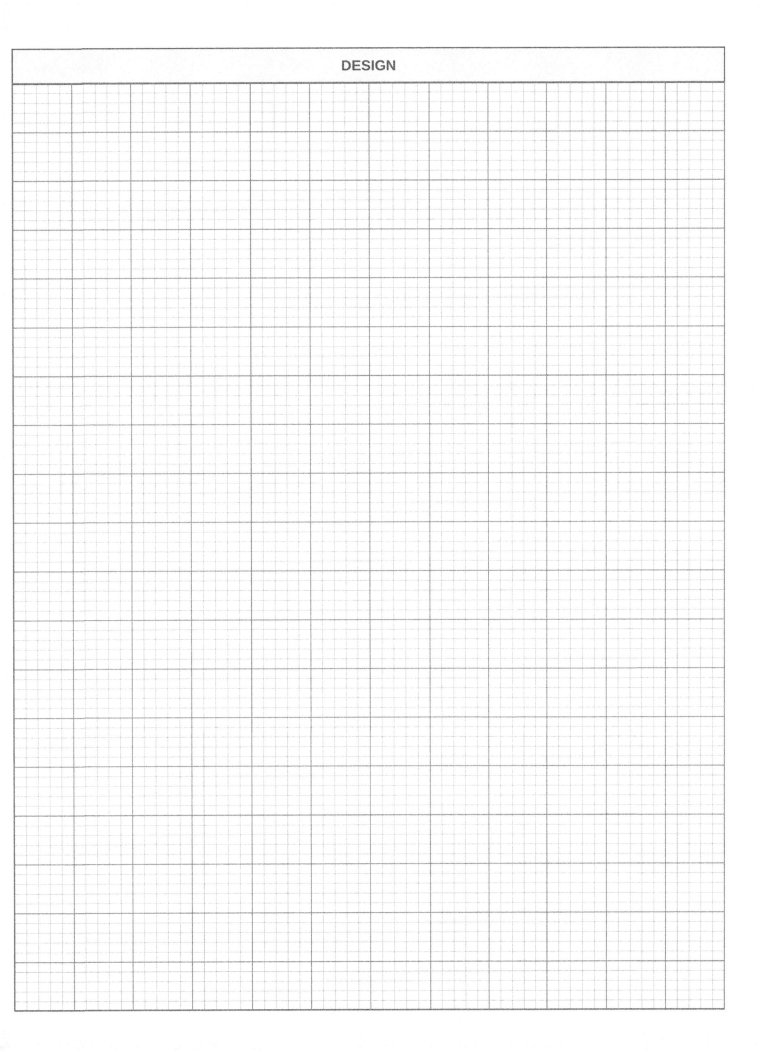

Project Name _____

Project No.

Who I'm making it for _____

Occasion _____

Date started _____ Date finished _____

SKETCH

NOTES

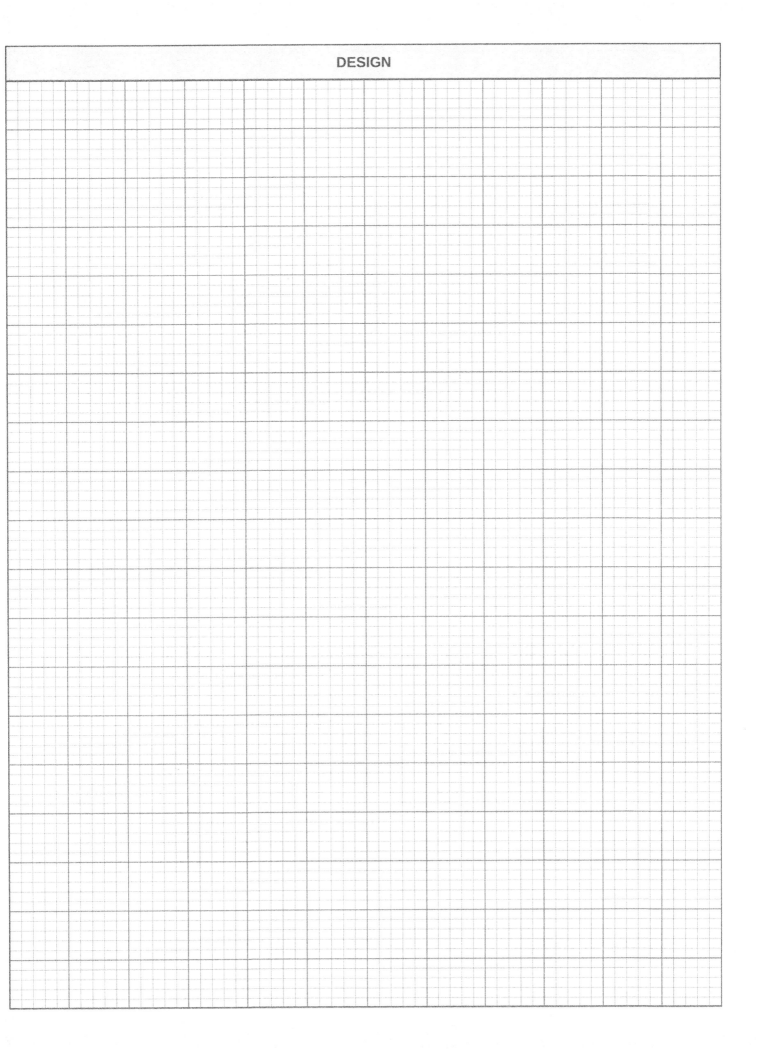

Project Name _____

Who I'm making it for _____

Occasion _____

Date started _____ Date finished _____

Project No.

SKETCH

NOTES

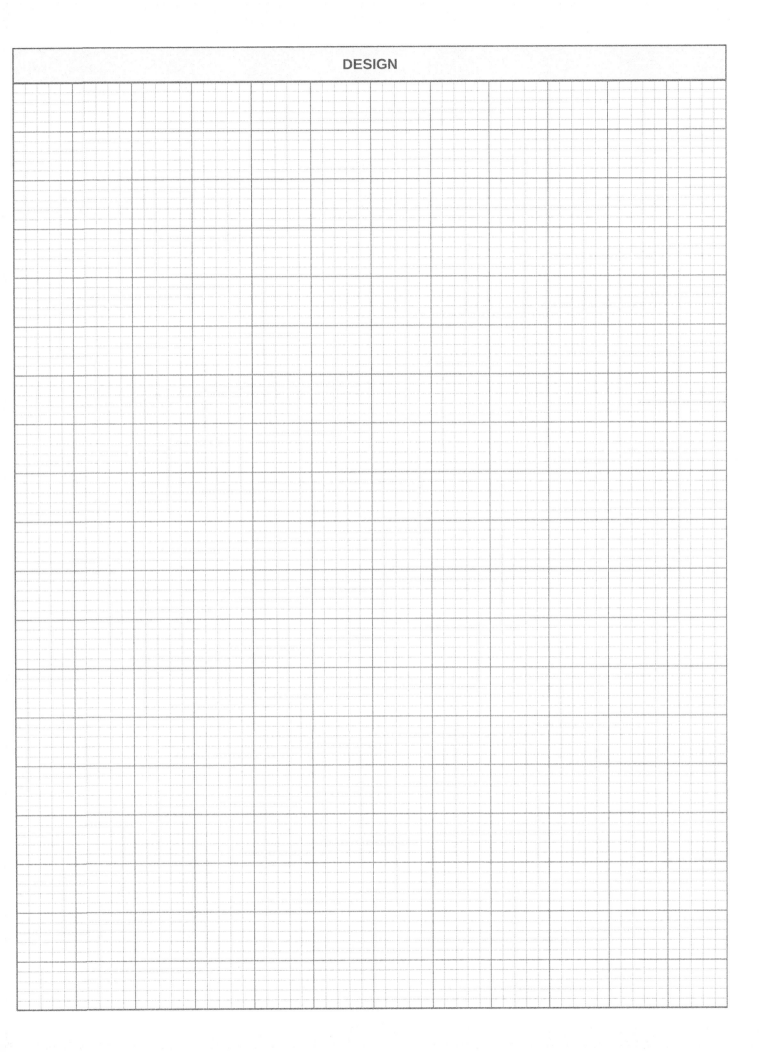

Project Name _____

Project No.

Who I'm making it for _____

Occasion _____

Date started _____ Date finished _____

SKETCH

NOTES

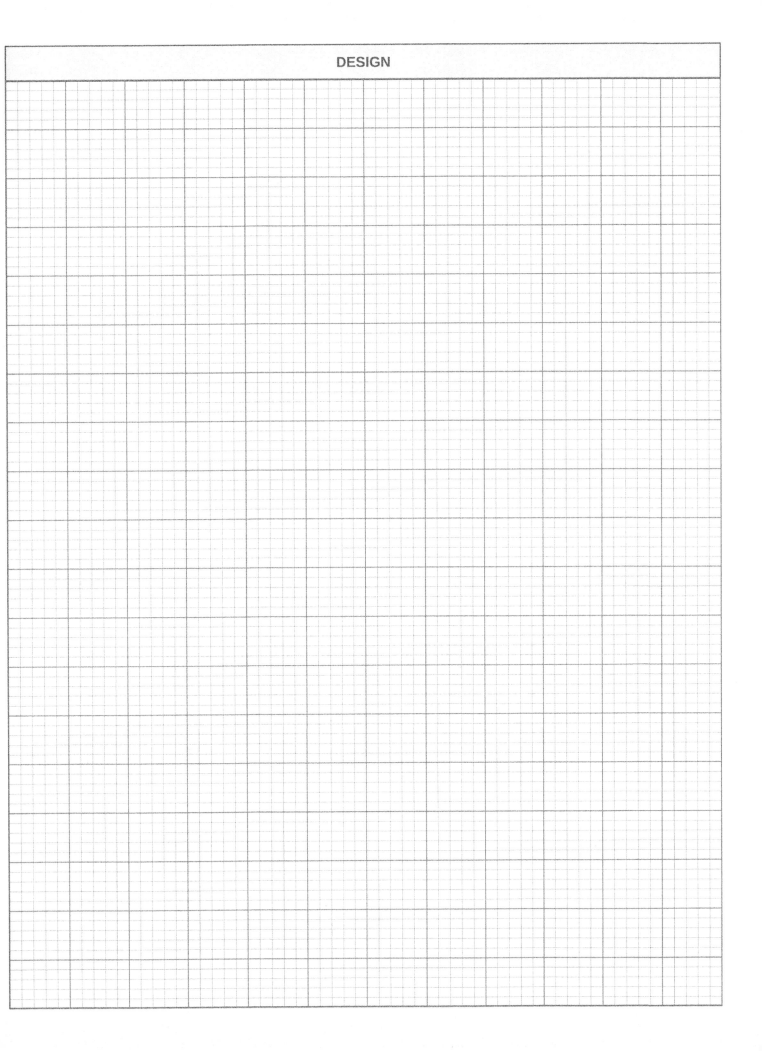

Project Name _____

Project No.

Who I'm making it for _____

Occasion _____

Date started _____ Date finished _____

SKETCH

NOTES

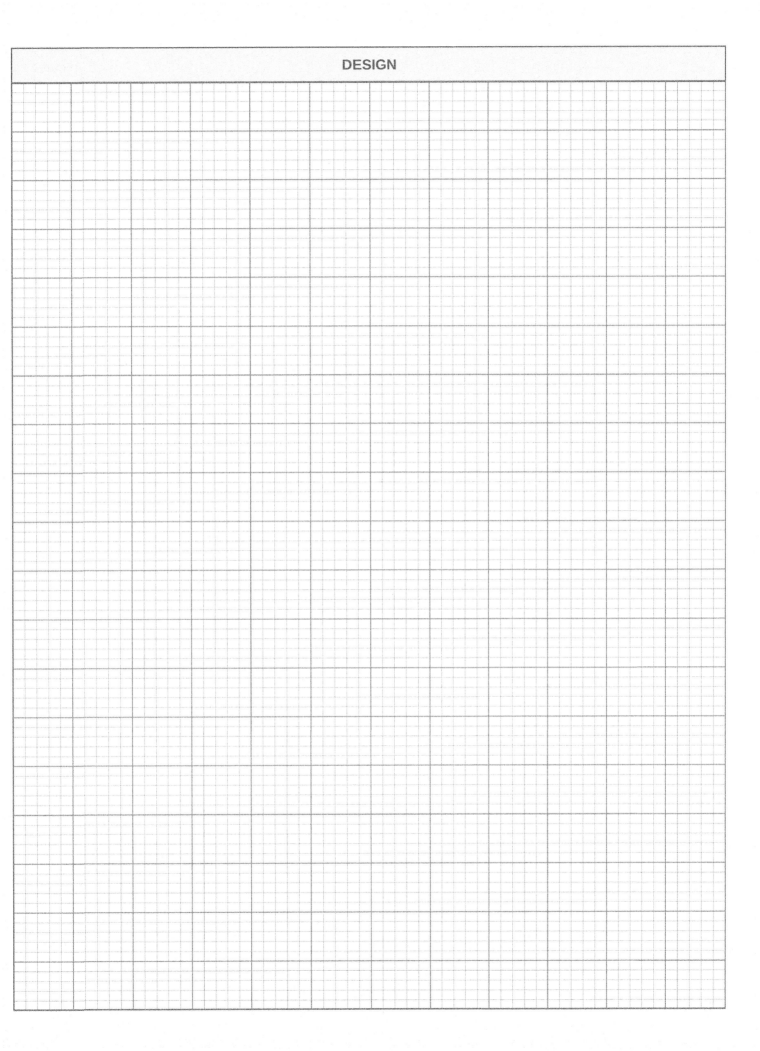

Project Name _____

Project No.

Who I'm making it for _____

Occasion _____

Date started _____ Date finished _____

SKETCH

NOTES

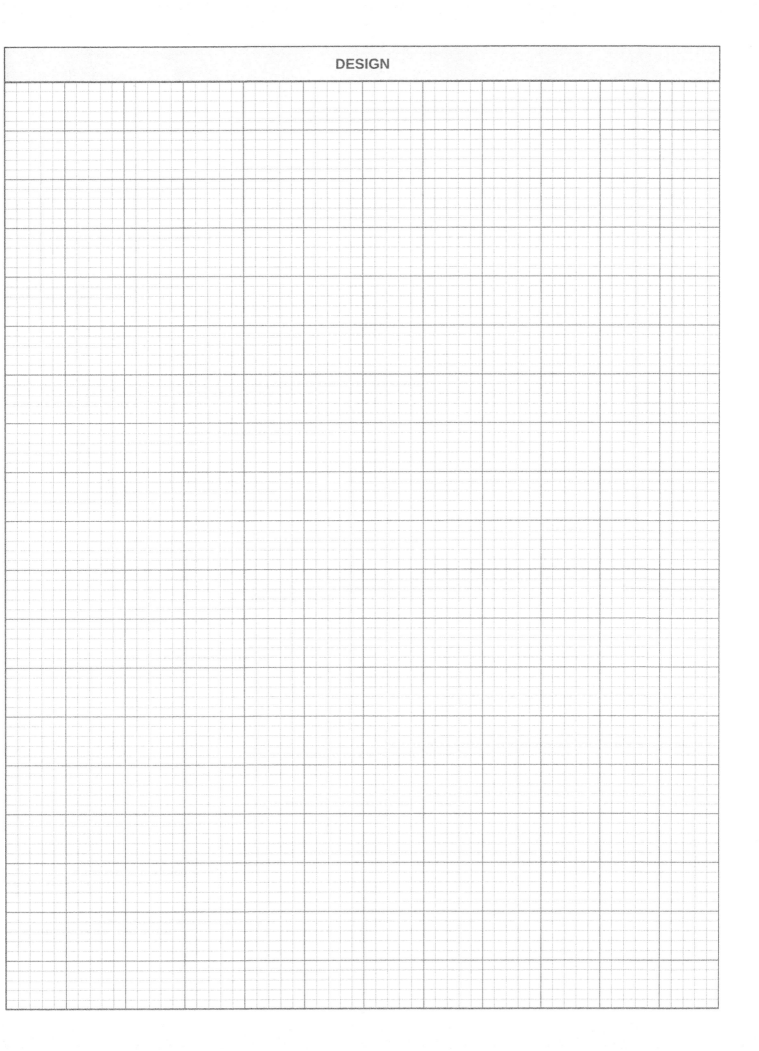

Project Name _____

	Project No.

Who I'm making it for _____

Occasion _____

Date started _____   Date finished _____

SKETCH

NOTES

Project Name _____

Project No.

Who I'm making it for _____

Occasion _____

Date started _____   Date finished _____

SKETCH

NOTES

Project Name _____

Project No.

Who I'm making it for _____

Occasion _____

Date started _____ Date finished _____

SKETCH

NOTES

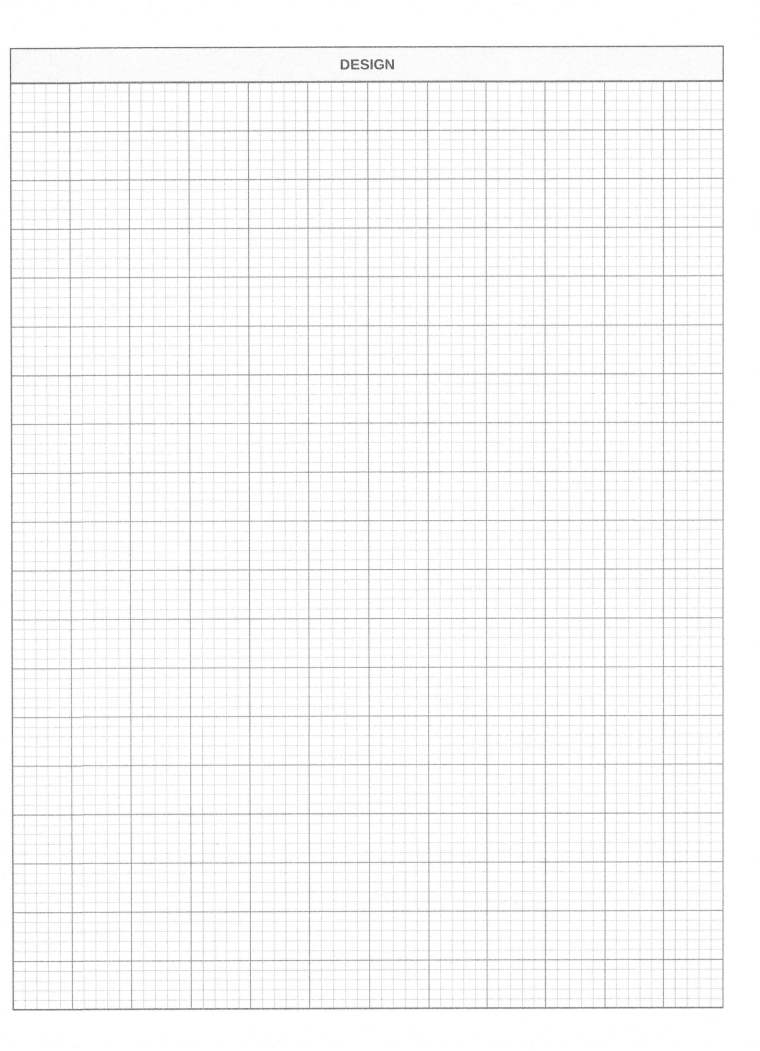

Project Name _____

Project No.

Who I'm making it for _____

Occasion _____

Date started _____ Date finished _____

SKETCH

NOTES

Project Name _____

Project No.

Who I'm making it for _____

Occasion _____

Date started _____ Date finished _____

SKETCH

NOTES

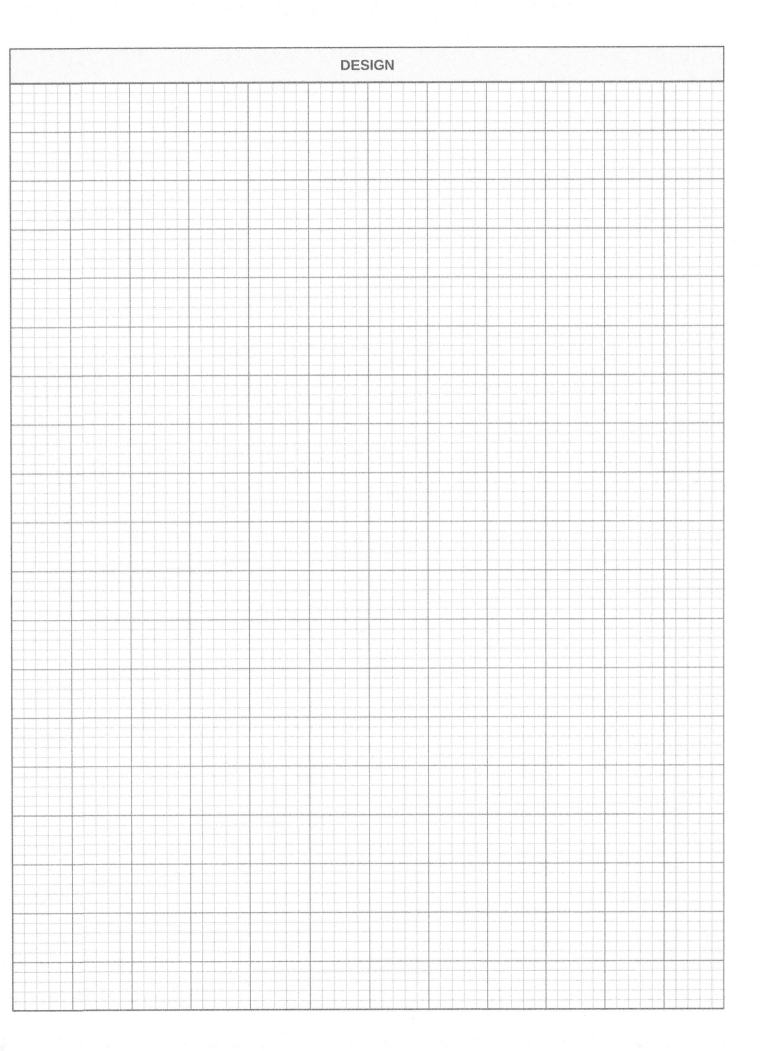

Project Name _____

Project No.

Who I'm making it for _____

Occasion _____

Date started _____ Date finished _____

SKETCH

NOTES

Project Name _____

Project No.

Who I'm making it for _____

Occasion _____

Date started _____   Date finished _____

SKETCH

NOTES

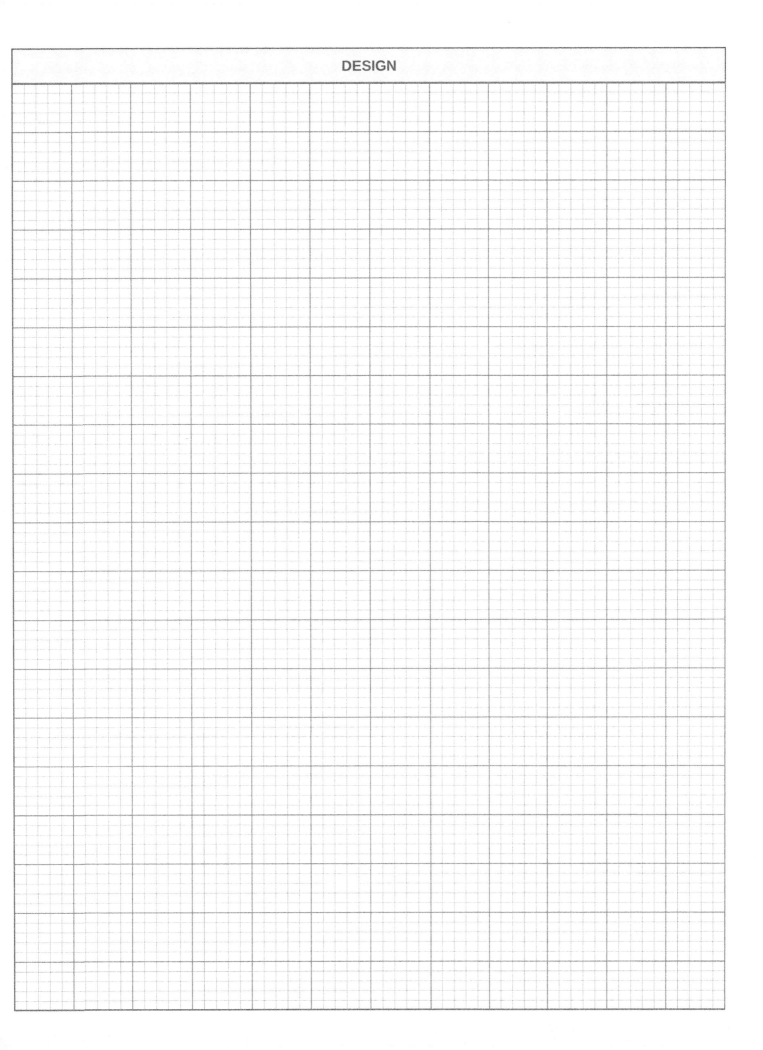

DESIGN

Project Name _____

Who I'm making it for _____

Occasion _____

Date started _____ Date finished _____

SKETCH

NOTES

Project Name _____

Who I'm making it for _____

Occasion _____

Date started _____ Date finished _____

SKETCH

NOTES

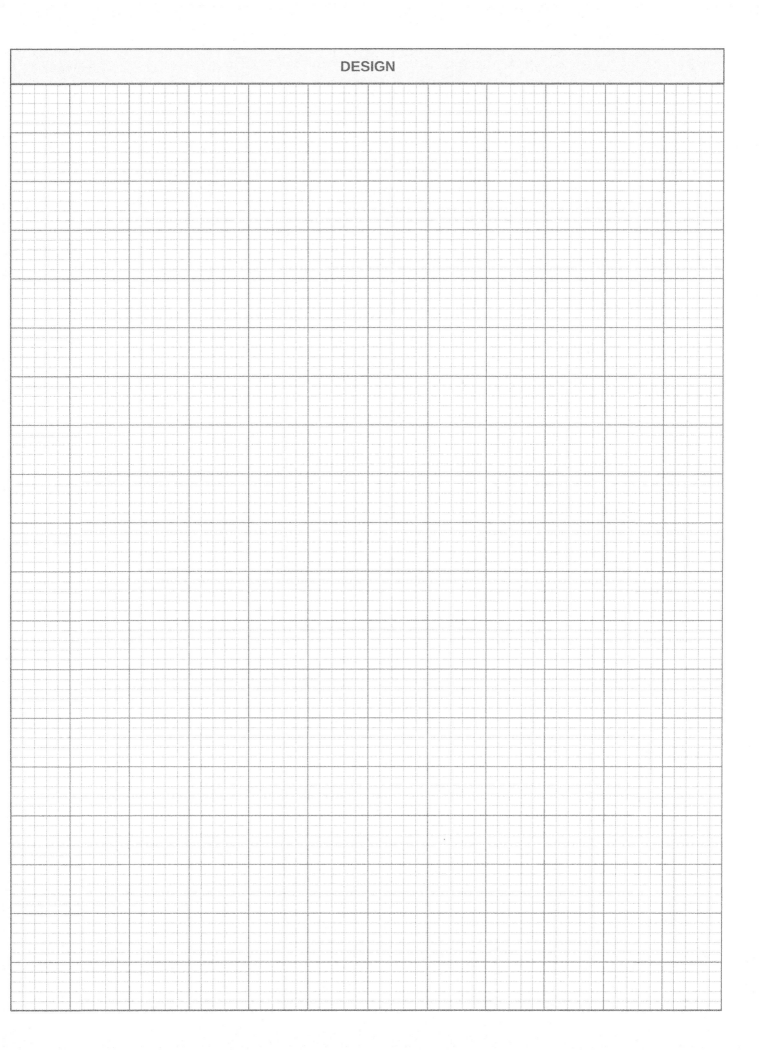

Project Name _____

Who I'm making it for _____

Occasion _____

Date started _____ Date finished _____

SKETCH

NOTES

Project Name _____

Who I'm making it for _____

Occasion _____

Date started _____ Date finished _____

SKETCH

NOTES

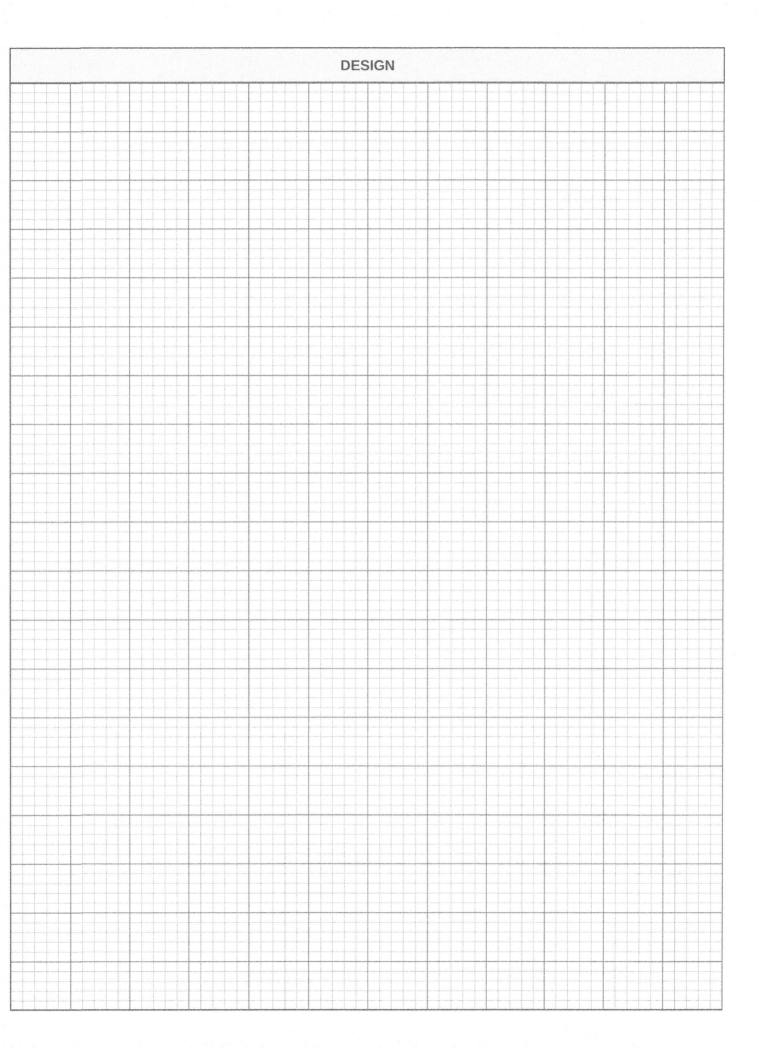

Project Name _____

Who I'm making it for _____

Occasion _____

Date started _____   Date finished _____

SKETCH

NOTES

Project Name _____

Project No.

Who I'm making it for _____

Occasion _____

Date started _____ Date finished _____

SKETCH

NOTES

Project Name _____

Project No.

Who I'm making it for _____

Occasion _____

Date started _____   Date finished _____

SKETCH

NOTES

Project Name _____

Project No.

Who I'm making it for _____

Occasion _____

Date started _____ Date finished _____

SKETCH

NOTES

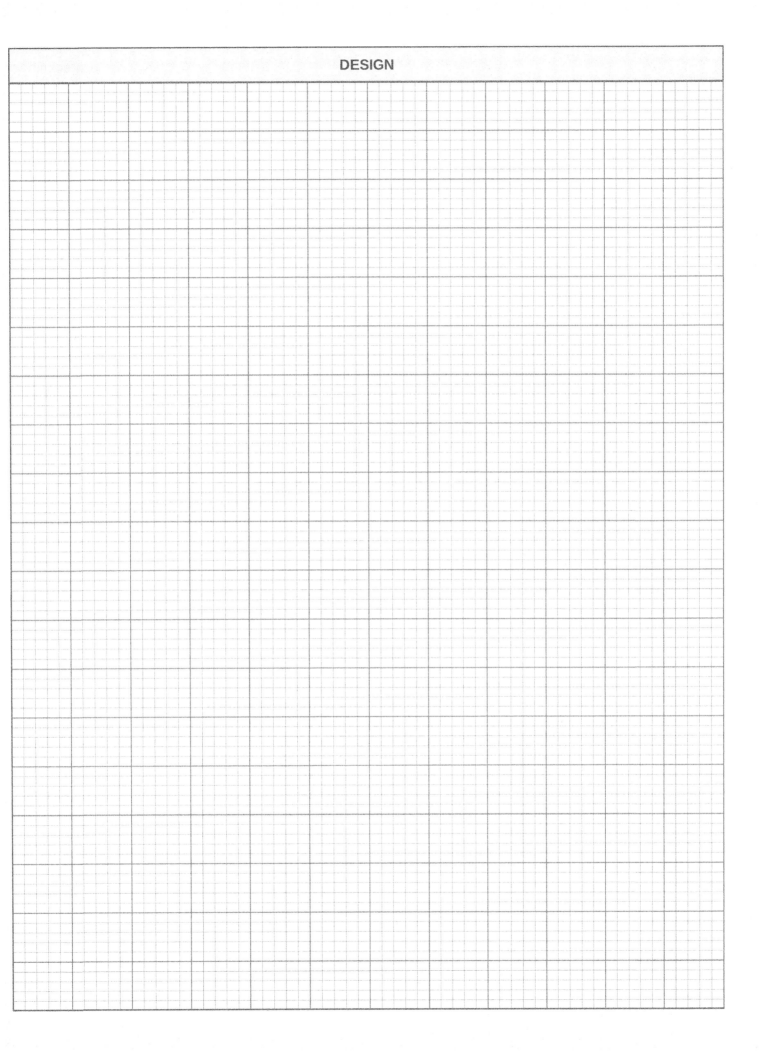

Project Name _____

Who I'm making it for _____

Occasion _____

Date started _____   Date finished _____

SKETCH

NOTES

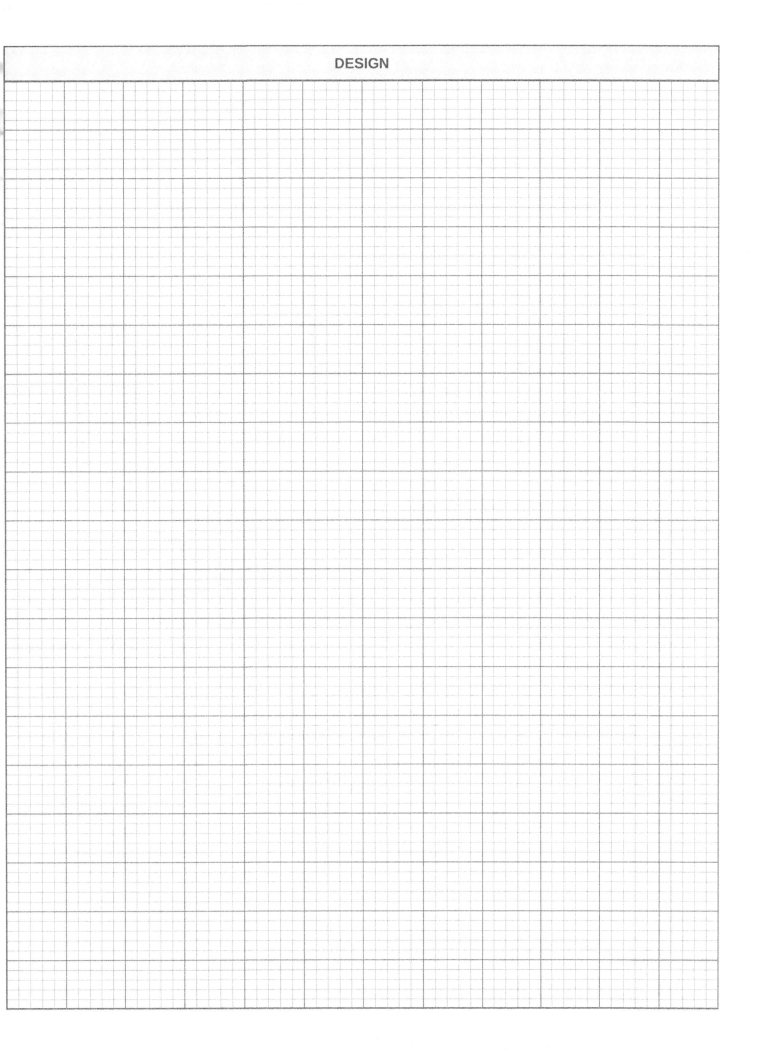

Project Name _____

Who I'm making it for _____

Occasion _____

Date started _____ Date finished _____

SKETCH

NOTES

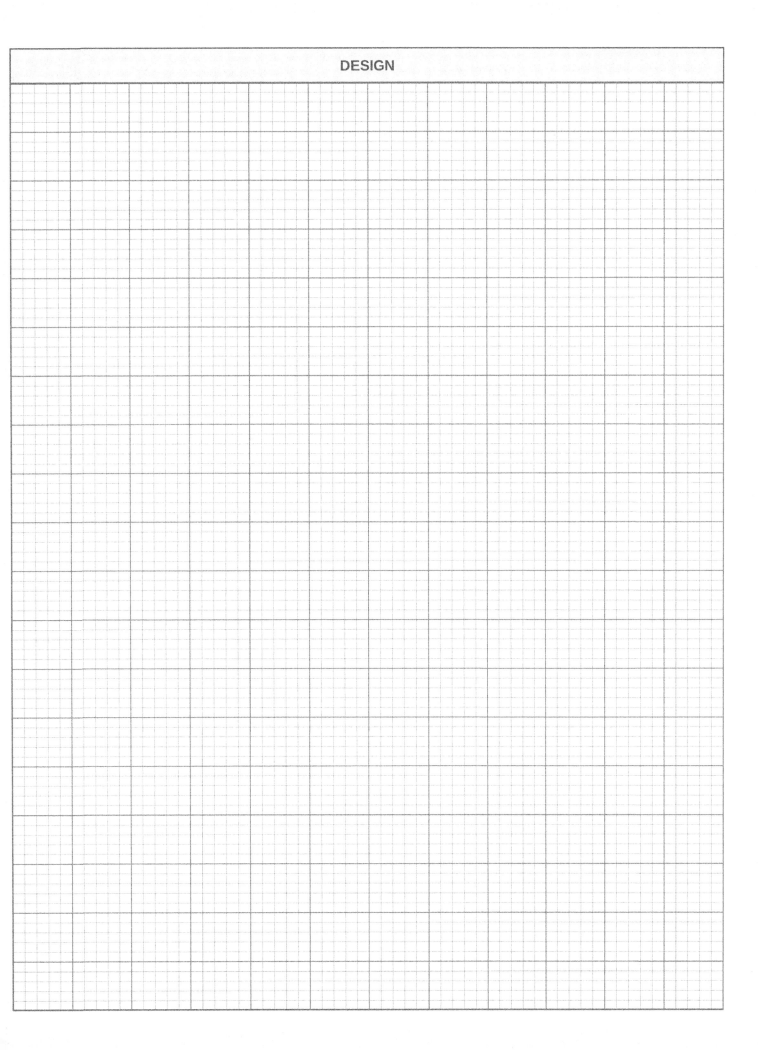

Project Name _____

Who I'm making it for _____

Occasion _____

Date started _____   Date finished _____

SKETCH

NOTES

Project Name _____

Project No.

Who I'm making it for _____

Occasion _____

Date started _____ Date finished _____

SKETCH

NOTES

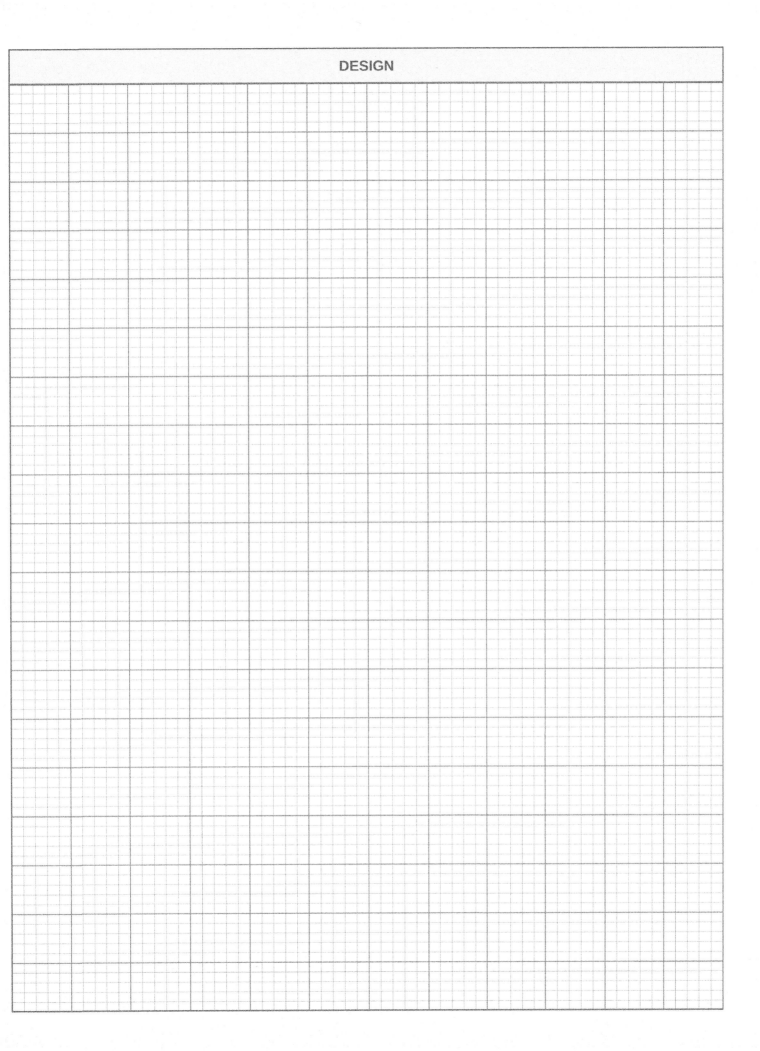

Project Name _____

Who I'm making it for _____

Occasion _____

Date started _____ Date finished _____

SKETCH

NOTES

Project Name _____

Who I'm making it for _____

Occasion _____

Date started _____ Date finished _____

SKETCH

NOTES

DESIGN

Project Name _____

Project No.

Who I'm making it for _____

Occasion _____

Date started _____ Date finished _____

SKETCH

NOTES

Project Name _____

Project No.

Who I'm making it for _____

Occasion _____

Date started _____ Date finished _____

SKETCH

NOTES

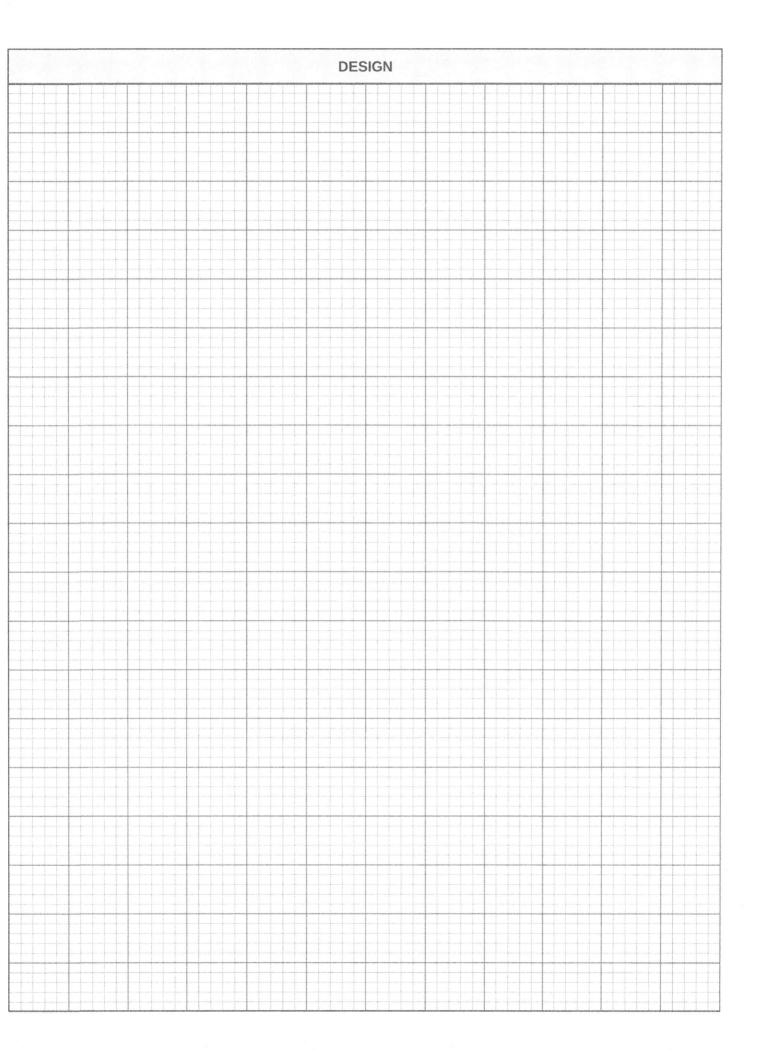

Project Name _____

Project No.

Who I'm making it for _____

Occasion _____

Date started _____ Date finished _____

SKETCH

NOTES

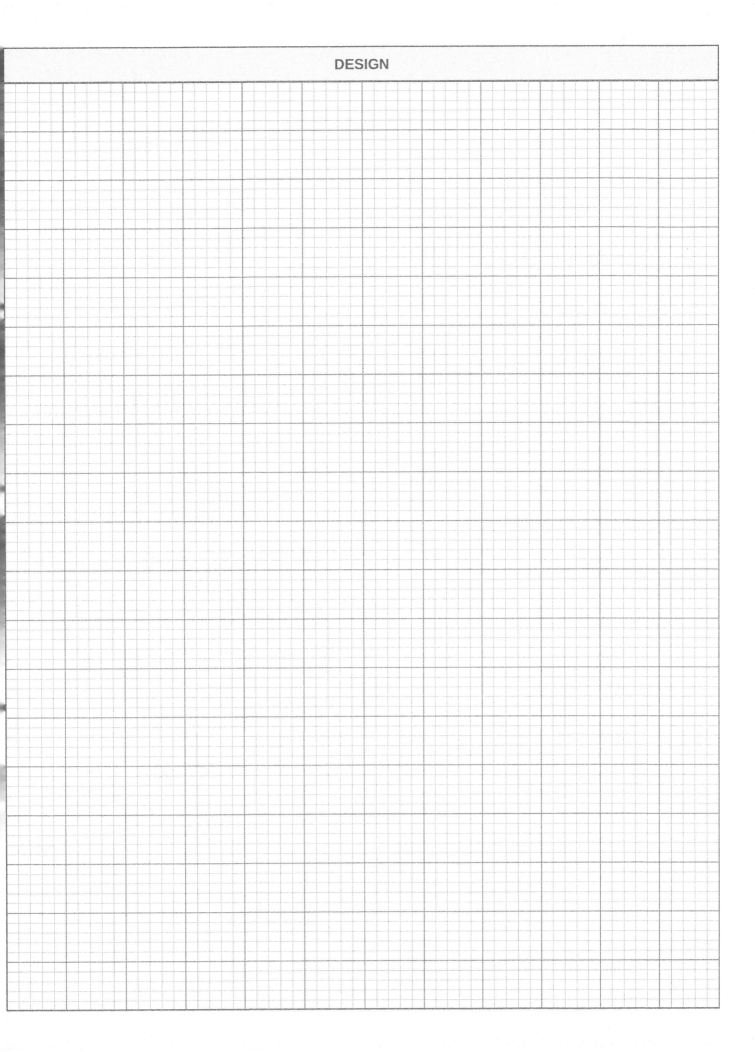

Project Name _____

Project No.

Who I'm making it for _____

Occasion _____

Date started _____ Date finished _____

SKETCH

NOTES

Project Name _____

Project No.

Who I'm making it for _____

Occasion _____

Date started _____ Date finished _____

SKETCH

NOTES

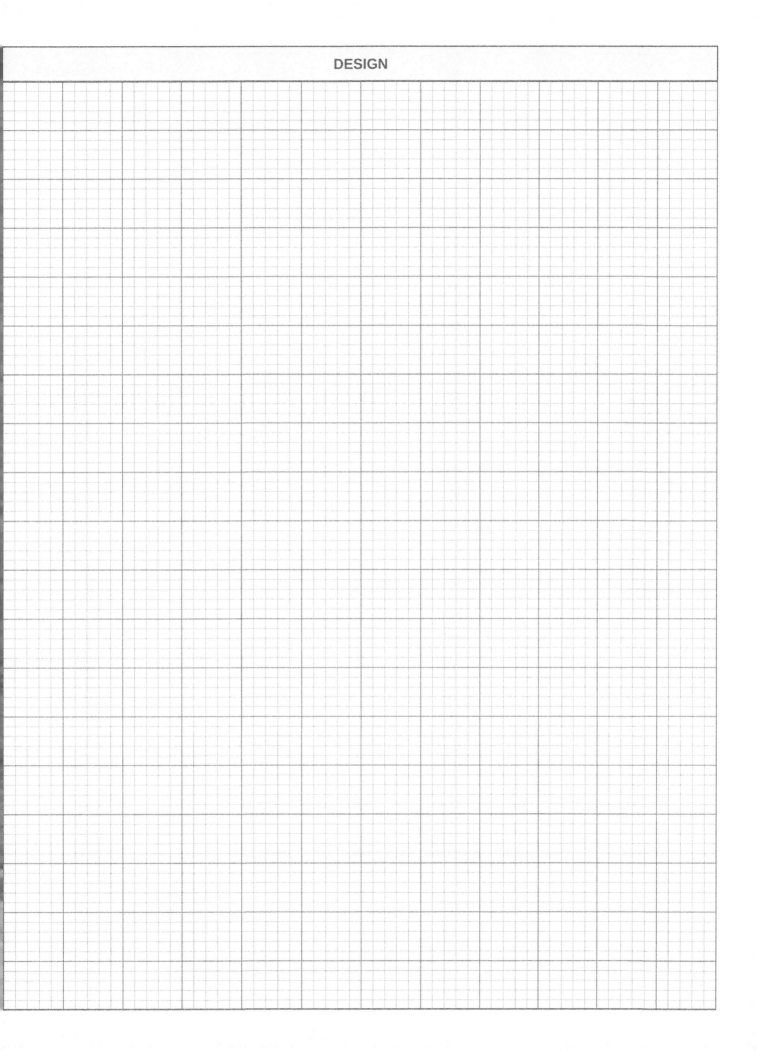

Project Name _____

Project No.

Who I'm making it for _____

Occasion _____

Date started _____ Date finished _____

SKETCH

NOTES

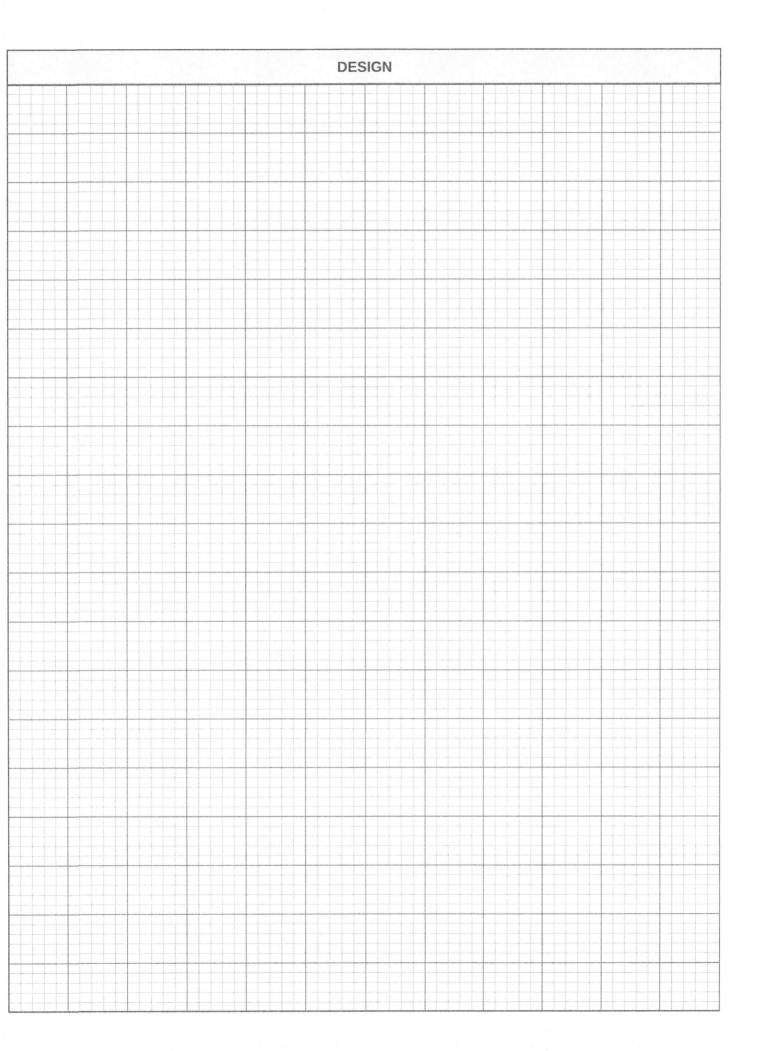

DESIGN

Project Name _____

Project No.

Who I'm making it for _____

Occasion _____

Date started _____ Date finished _____

SKETCH

NOTES

Project Name _____

Project No.

Who I'm making it for _____

Occasion _____

Date started _____ Date finished _____

SKETCH

NOTES

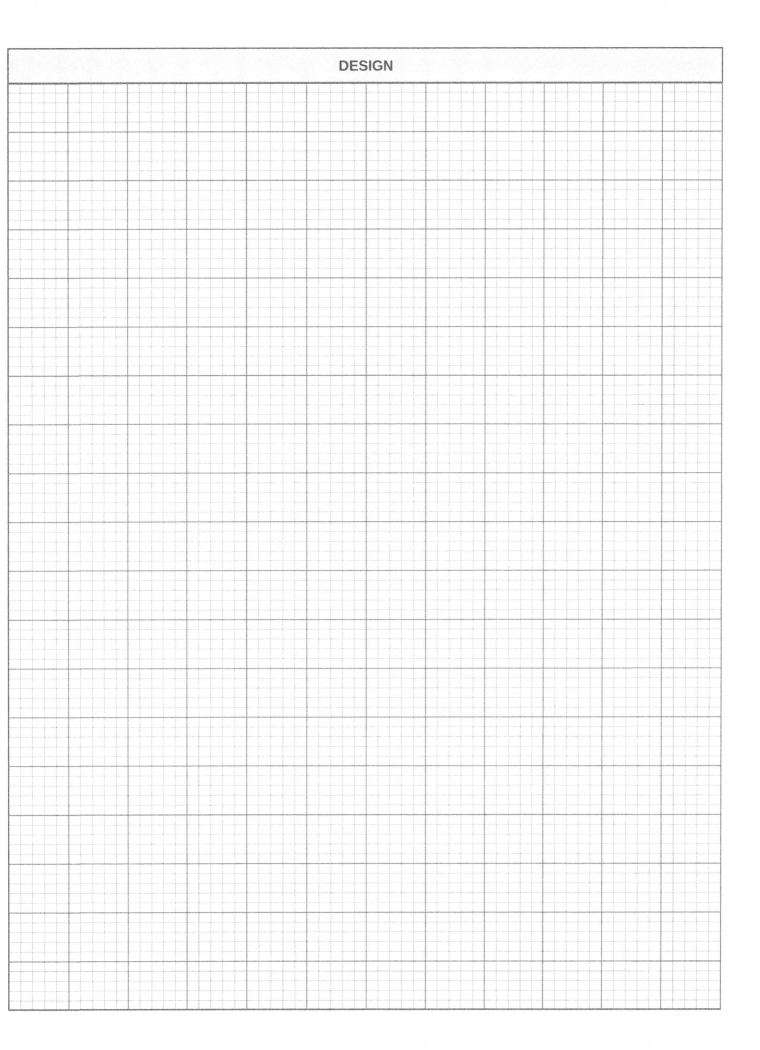

	Project No.
Project Name _____	

Who I'm making it for _____

Occasion _____

Date started _____ Date finished _____

SKETCH

NOTES

Project Name _____

Project No.

Who I'm making it for _____

Occasion _____

Date started _____ Date finished _____

SKETCH

NOTES

	Project No.
Project Name _____	

Who I'm making it for _____

Occasion _____

Date started _____ Date finished _____

SKETCH

NOTES

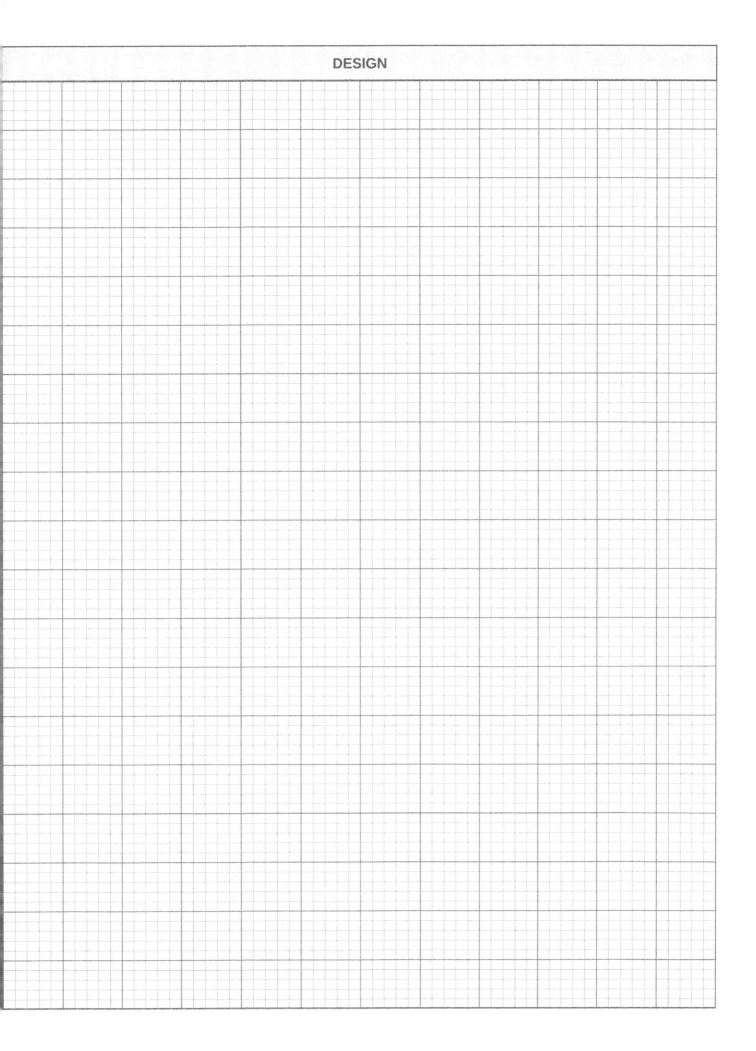

Project Name _____

	Project No.

Who I'm making it for _____

Occasion _____

Date started _____ Date finished _____

SKETCH

NOTES

Project No.

Project Name _____

Who I'm making it for _____

Occasion _____

Date started _____ Date finished _____

SKETCH

NOTES

Project Name _____

Project No.

Who I'm making it for _____

Occasion _____

Date started _____ Date finished _____

SKETCH

NOTES

Project Name _____

Project No.

Who I'm making it for _____

Occasion _____

Date started _____ Date finished _____

SKETCH

NOTES

Project Name _____

Project No.

Who I'm making it for _____

Occasion _____

Date started _____ Date finished _____

SKETCH

NOTES

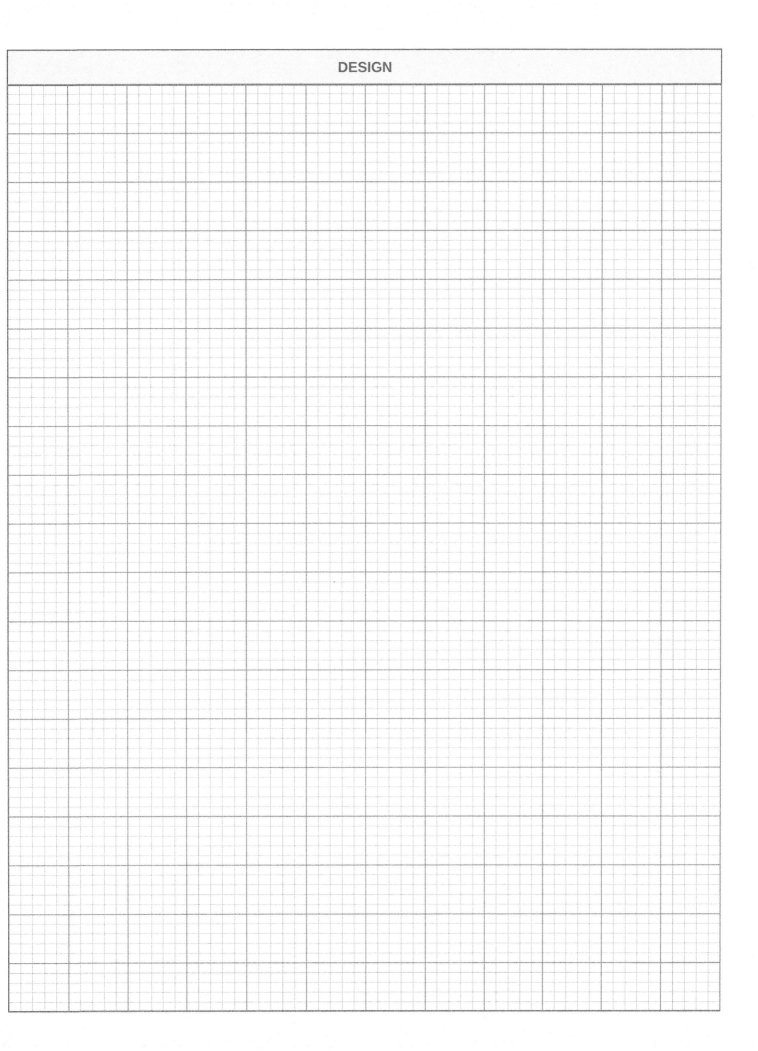

Project Name _____

Who I'm making it for _____

Occasion _____

Date started _____ Date finished _____

SKETCH

NOTES

Project Name _____

Project No.

Who I'm making it for _____

Occasion _____

Date started _____ Date finished _____

SKETCH

NOTES

Made in the USA
Las Vegas, NV
15 August 2022

53286516R00063